The World for
Wedding Ring

The World for Wedding Ring

Poems by Daniel Berrigan, S.J.

The Macmillan Company–New York

MACMILLAN NEW YORK, LONDON

Imprimi potest   *Nihil obstat*
  James Shanahan, S.J.   Edward J. Montano, S.T.D.
  January 20, 1962   Censor Librorum

Imprimatur
  ✠ Francis Cardinal Spellman
  Archbishop of New York
  August 1, 1962

Some of these poems originally appeared in *America,*
The American Scholar, Commonweal, Crosslight, Poetry,
Spirit, Thought, and *Unity.*

First Printing

The Macmillan Company, New York
Collier-Macmillan Canada, Ltd., Galt, Ontario
Divisions of The Crowell-Collier Publishing Company

Printed in The United States of America

Library of Congress catalog card number: 62-19418

Designed by Hermann Strohbach

DOROTHY DAY
TONY WALSH
KARL MEYER

beati pauperes spiritu
beati pacifici

CONTENTS

1 | The World

I | The World

HOPE

All night the fretful cricket

skirrs like a conscience, night in his bones
light in his points of eye—hope

illiterate and fey,
a cock rousing miniscule dawn

match flare might make, or a candle end
and he foolish cry *dawn!* at the false dawn

that prowled him out for death.

How small a thing is hope—
hairspring body, mind's eye, and all endangered.

LANDSCAPES THERE ARE

    of such formal will and silken atmosphere,
one seeks in lower corner the legendary Chinese
his brush drawing him gently into stillness.

Not conquest of height
matters, nor grandiose will
but an uncopyable phrase

a heart's errand, a bough in one direction
running.
            Like a child's legend or man's death
or *I love you,* never in history repeating itself.

EVENTS

Events are orthodoxy, he would say,
submitting like any son.
The way a fruit tastes of itself
he tasted sacrifice.
No thirst but for that cup
engendering thirst.

Truest credo is event, would say
and said it to a brother's face
by birth or death brought near—
a descending god he saw, a god
sprung from his tears.
Piety of experience
bound him in web.
He wore the world for wedding band.

Here
A few notes toward a life.
Words, words are what we buried.

Look; time wears new features, time takes heart.

Moon

Battlements, tombs—no longer
populous or loud, the living
towns go underground.
The impalpable dead are come.
All Souls' cock on the steeple
summons them out of doors
to touch autumnal hands
to breathe the estranging air.
Toward false dawn they renounce
abulia and death;
passionate, bodied, cry;
whey-faced people of light
cannot abide. But black
is beautiful at last.
Dark, dark be the spell. Public
man never made love.
Grow him a dark grove.

TIME AT HEART

Trees on the avenue prosper;
thoughtful, tall as prophets, bent
over the spectacle of youth and age.

Mornings, young mothers lift children from prams
to creep after grandfather sun

evenings, old men and women hear
all down that height, heart like a prophecy

(they grope for one another, hand or face)

time at heart of the oak makes more than leaves to fall

GHOSTS

Perhaps Beatrice, no more
than a spirit's breath. Or Christ,
presentment of bread and wine. You cannot know
if you love only the living.

Men
descend among dead men, remount
through ivory gates, thereafter search
in converse other voices, in eyes other eyes—

they walk carefully as they bore a vessel
brimming mystery. *You are, but more
contain.*

A FORTIETH YEAR

Nothing portentous. But recall
shame for half a heart, a cheapside ghost; recall
what dull edge the truth wears to
on stony minds.

The better wars the good, a fratricide.
Doctrinaire, red with zeal
men drown the human in a sacred stream
and generate, row on row, eyeless faces
out of this world. The waters hurry past
to drown polluted use.

Others
if mind gave up its dead
if the dead spoke, must hear footsteps
shaking that sea. A judgment—
how men die there, cannot lie there.
If skulls spin
witless north by northeast,
fish are their radiants,
their lightning tongues schooled in one name
to bear men home.
But there, there
they rot, not rise.

The Sacraments Are on Behalf of Man

The people, men and women together
clasp hands and turn home away.
They will sit at bread and beer, and make love
having prayed Jesus Christ dutifully

who was, say their joined hands, their bodies,
man, boy in the house, burden
in woman's body. So eye to eye we read his text
in ours. And hear in those pages

his voice, brief of speech
long and enduring in love. I could set tonguing
like a shire of bells in time's constant wind

the widow's son arisen, the thousands fed—

By one garden tomb
whose dust cries out *He is not here*

even the world is borne.

THE EFFORT OF UNDERSTANDING

Look up.
To claim the air as that hawk does—
even as image, fatuous.
At such height, earth is a poor
glomerate of no smells, no elbows. I had rather
here.
     But there sometimes
catch breath, dwelling in his eyes—
what does he, what would I, know?

WINTER UPON OUR EYES

    do the dead endure, eyeless and stern
sleepwalking their dark cities?

                           Autumn leads
within heart. Midwinter, refusal
of all but ghosts, makes man seem
dun shadow of true man, unmelded
palette of that splendor
awaits him.

                A sere Christ
clings the stripped tree. His mouth
if winds are oracle to him or no
is shaped to
               come

SUN

We run toward flesh
when it cries, crossing ours
I thirst. But this? he perishes
Lucifer, of no flesh.

Christ's blood flaring
at dawn, means
fair weather for us. But this?
he fails, falls from height.

We could not, but for hope
live night through.
But who lights his dark
declivities?

Straw flare, straw man
love brands, like
man's kiss or cross, your brow of hell.

THE LENS

Poignant, this counterpoint—
young lives unwrung by their world
and fretful poplars, enduring the season's
gradual death blow,
exposed root and musculature
huddling for last stand.

Young faces counterpoint
faces time grinds so hard and clear—
your lens, young John and Margaret.

But who sees youth going? it is here
or never. I cannot, for all of love
bind in one healing image
the scabrous blind limbs of trees
and the supple hands, eyed and sensuous
that break and stack old bones of trees
a hecatomb, a night picnic fire.

MORTALITY

A leaf's falling tells
or morning red or evening grey

which of two mingling airs
blue or blue, time or eternity

color old eyes. Tells
if flesh melts

like snowman under time's fire; or bones stand
clumsy and crutched, March trees waiting—

flesh a flowering cherry, blood a May wine.

A WONDER OF ORIGINS;

                    flower points to a bird,
bird cries like a closed eye *I see your dreams.*

Things like my heart I never see, but see
hearts bird-shaped, flower-shaped, the radiant

weightless shadow my heart casts—upward,
to ground; a rose, a wintering bird.

They meet, they summer
plummet and signet, in Hero's hand.

MIDWINTER

Unmoving light,
plowed fields, contours under snow
lightly scarred over, an arrested use—

time unleafed, time fruitless
black pigment on white, a skeleton
future will flesh out—

insists on no blessing, offers
slight resistance to eternity

as Eurydice in death held fast
no more than winter tree its leaves, to life; no more
than fields their stripped harvest, to him—

went mildly childlike, hand in hand with great death

lightly resisting, or not at all, eternity.

Tree

It takes measure of man
and builds him parables—one for every wind
and one for silence
which the necessitous heart requires.

So heart's dulled edge, mind's lessening arc
calamitous old age
are unexplainably sweetened.

A dusty hedgerow bird
clings there, blazes
a beggared savior.

The Poem Waits on Experience

    a ghost in offstage darkness; no lines,
no wig, no eyes. I have not loved the poor,
I have not died yet.

Yet I am poor
as all the shanties of the world
gone up in one flare;
on a rotted springs
a junky's baked skeleton.

Here, for its worth, the poem.

STYLE

    envelops a flower like its odor;
bestows on radiant air
the spontaneous word that greets and makes a king.

Tragic too, where man walks—
a long shadow at evening isolates
all he is not.

SECOND THOUGHTS

November moon is malfeasance.
His eye is knives; a death of flowers,
of marriages.
           For all *I take you*
a malaise now;
           I told you so

SONG

The mind's life I sing, the subtle unageing humor
that poured in nostril and ear, raises the dead.
The heart's life, whose symbol is cormorant, hart.
Imagination that shakes the tame world
as thought grows blooded and particular

So after death, the clear yes of existence
like a forest burning foxes fed on,
a plain of shins and thighs
a word could leaf out, and would, green again.

THE LEVITE

A thousand-year-old corpse has no redress;
it hearkens, sybilline,

undistracted, head upon breast.
In that confessional guise, all is his grist,

whose blood is rust, whose body
clings like a locust shell its tree.

We read the image. One hour,
one afternoon, and we are signatory

of guilt and guilt expunged. We and our fathers
roundelay about this pole

airing an argument which unopposed
we win, you lose.

Simply, though under wormwood
under old nails and joists, under

a stroke of ancient style that isolates
like time's genius, your visionary gift—

though the cost is in us by need compounded,
a calculus of time—

yet, we beseech, have done
let the stretched arms have done

stretched loins, drained heart, all
their tragic charade. The dead may come

their task done, into resurrection—
an hour, a transcendent hush

a stranger's face at door, a voice,
unfaltering hands upon our evening bread.

11 | For Wedding Ring

Awakening

When I grew appalled by love
and promised nothing, but stood, a sick man
first time on feeble knees
peering at walls and weather
like the feeble-minded—
the strange outdoors, the house of strangers—
there, there was a beginning.

The world peeled away
usual upon usual
like foil in a fire.
Fell that day, all summer
a dying Gaul
his blood around, his naked beauty.
That day, mind made an elegy
world might gape at and weep.

I forget it now.
But remember too; a green tree
all winter's ignorant winds trampled in vain.

THE POET AS OBSERVER

I sit like a dunce in the incandescent noon
on a high stool, in a cone cap, and make notes

a liberated blind man
whose eyes bear him like wings
out of night's stinking nest, into this world.

Intellectual vision, reality by definition?
No. The Jesuit mind, a Homer

assembles fleets, sails for its continent
across seas tamed by the ordering governing glance.

But to light on and finger the world, bit by bit
an old woman in the flea market—

junk, onions, ordure. Ingredients and parts.
The old fingers, wise as eyes, come on something. A yes.

LAZARUS

–I–

Silence rolled over and over my body its
monstrous milling, till a fine dust
settled on millstone death.
If truth were told, the white dust could not tell it
even when that young Magian
cried *open-sesame* and puffed me to a man.

Lazarus

—II—

After my universe was only
two sisters above me, and they murmuring
gradual farewell, like bells or heartbeat—

I could not care, nor summon
to whisper *I do not care.* Yet for them
my heart stood like a stricken drummer: one beat more.

And I take breath to cry; *it was not death!*
Though his steps slower fell than the great stone,
he had said, said, *I am the way*

and banished death away
chiding
from the stone doorway, away their tears.

HAVING ENDURED THE DEAD

   the original poor of all
who without hands trouble the house
who without eyes
darken the world's fraudulent show

having endured the dead

who without appetite moil the night's lust
laugh it to black scorn   a toothless hound's laughter

having endured the dead.

Last night Russ Whalen's death
struck us in face, his friends.

You bore it hardest, who move for years now
on rotting Young Street. *Poor man*
the poor named you; they forgave
Christ for your sake.

For only recompense
old age, illness. Behind a crooked shutter
death's blear look
takes your measure too, waiting day out.

              (*for Tony Walsh*)

GRANDFATHER POEM

What men desire
passionately or in rumination
he would let go

discarding body
today, tomorrow,
a chance hook for an odd thing,

closing eyes as sun goes
a thousand times, then once
for all, named death.

Semblance first, then evidence—
see in old eyes
lucid now, a night
no enterprise, no cloud may stain.

THE LABOR

A declarative. Man
is infantile, until a father's hand

draw lamprey mouth away
from long lactation, a false peace at breast.

A simple eye makes man. Laborious hands
elucidate the heart, that otherwise

thwarted and died, an idling
beggar under his father's stair.

viable imagination comes of seven labors.
Include hell in that passage, return

to worlds dense as a Grecian pass
with man's hope; *the unsmoking flame, intact?*

To Wallace Stevens

In each of us you live on, the lodged seed
of empiric imagination
from a great pod blown on death's virile wind.

You live in us; a life, creating dangers,
toppling the platitudes
that sink in mind and heart their flat denials.

Credo, we said, *credo,* mirror
to mirror, an inhumanity
before no god.

You are our puzzle. You, naked as we
amid the poverties of our world
—flowers, donkeys, angels meek as water—
cunningly
surpassed us in an hour. Refusing our credo
your marvelous method
made dawn, made a world, made marriage of light and flesh

without God, you said. But is decree of absence
final, when the imagination yields
like a god's brow
godlike men, armed, passionate for their world?

MY MOTHER

I know love's
are large claims, but hers
modest as hands
whose eloquence must borrow—
a word, a flower, a child's face for instrument.

Even in dreams, hands speak for her.
Speak?
Creation is summons. Their speech creates
awakenings.

Two Days After Death

It is too soon for poems;
I write down in clumsy grief
Mary's unlettered face

never by sun and air, our elements
to flourish like bay tree, to be our ornament
to light the winter scape, our kings' incense
our fiery child on bitter January night

never. I walk past
winter trees plunged upright,
an iron world. Breathe
like swords, the zero air of loss.

1 9 6 1

I summon my parents, a jubilee morning.
When in gold vestments I came down
to kiss them where they stood, their tears and mine

were a clear pressing of the eighty-year vine.
I touched their faces, a gentle unweathered grain
the blind might visualize, as of green leaves
up from exposed ground.
                         What winter fury
that moment tempered, they and I know.

ON THE SUBLIME

That mind bleakly human
that heart crowned by death's ironies—

see, He submits

to purple patch, clumsy hands and minds
as though
to serve a mind's expedient vision
were God's heart's wish.

Believe, it is. His victory
is dumb as ours, till man
have it by heart.

In Memoriam

–I–

Seldom, death's virulent fires fail—
disease, consuming effort of mind—
all or any, each an end.

No, but for once
clarify in act
their own defeat.

One harrowing profitless winter,
sun turned a blank page.
The world arose, illustration
of its own blackened magnificent form.

In Memoriam

–II–

A magisterial touch was firm
in the firm mouth turned toward silence, turned
on the making wheel of the world.

Time in its turning
lipped the clay lightly, taught it words
remembered for gentleness when a face recedes
to its stone image in an honored place.

SOUL TO BODY

The substance of things
goes deeper than a hand,
a courteous bookstand before the soul; or eyes
that, like candlelight, bring friends nearer

than night can. Yet eyes
are nearest mystery; glance
is a pebble falling all their depth. *Hear me.*
You started something time rings down unfinished.

Reliance is the soul's form.
Not cozening or spaniel
but *I will to need you. Without your steel*
I am supreme, but when will I taste blood?

I am creation, I am
every horizon, sea and
Everest. But who claims me, unless admiration light on
your flag's folds, your ships whose thirst

is my imprisoned urge?
Thought is a more
elevated presence, but without sweat, tears
tactic and danger, who could achieve

from throats that drank
only miles, only burning days—
Thermopylae, Lepanto?
                              We, we are here.
Now drink from helmet the chilled wine death.

I Love You

I see a procession of the old;
death shunts them on, pillar to post;

man and wife, hands clasped,
a piteous nobility.

That word comes now
through the mind's pain, into truth.

Mercy, forgiveness, *You are my heart's ground.*

HOMILY

I said, a cleric worth his salt
will salt his bread with tears, sometimes.
will break bread
which is the world's flesh, with the world's poor,
count this his privilege and more—

And called Saint Paul for exemplar
whose fingers stitched the church a robe,
its crude device
a Christ crucified, wrought of his workman's hands
which the foul dust had sealed
utter and unforeseen, priest and lord.

No disdain, I said, must stain the workman's hands
that such task own.
It is all one, I cried. The Lord
upbears the poor man's hand in His, His fruit.
Gospel has it so; one, grape, tendril, shoot and root.

The confession of humanity is our honor, clerics.
Celibate fatherhood—that irony
is a gestation time urges to term—
the heart's hung fruit, summering green as grass
is heart at last, red in the world's press.

You are the poor man's food.
Or great Burgundy, rotting, sours time's ground.

A Doge in Hell

I brought to that enterprise
a tepid will
that trimmed its tip, thought itself fiery
but in the world's atmosphere
faltered, a eunuch's tool.

Mere good will
populated earth, I thought, with men of will,
held them in fist, a doge's
five blazing fingers, a nest of light, a christendom.

And was I governor?
Gentlemen, time nudges
a sleeping hulk in vain, time prizes
stone lips apart, time time
cracks me like chestnuts, a puff, a rot.
Winds mock in high c
through life's interstices, the fop
that shivers in his iron nightshirt, pointing
wrong north for wanderer Christ.

I had sought
of all heaven's teeming cloth
that spreads, clean and unclean
the spirit's gustatory—one, one only
favorable auspex.

But lie stretched, a gutless flesh
on hell's spit, flesh to grow Cerberus
his eyes' envy, his tooth's sweat.

The battening dog
ribbed with my flesh, hot with my heart's wine
grins for his portrait in a doge's gown.

Good Caiphas

    perfumes, resin, nard—
they fell in showers
on fallen Christ.
We will make sandalwood of him
and store like bees
honey in his stern eyes.
Someone, ages gone
will touch a spring
and chant the open-sesame
and find our golden Pharaoh safe as wheat.

Or so they thought.
But blood, blood
writes red in memory
one name; and when dawn breaks
it wakens, and we cry—
is this the wasted vine
God's hand has healed,
pressed, poured, to warm the centuries' heart?

Flesh too from one dark loom
is ours and his, whole cloth.
When winds take him on high
we follow too.
That watchful hurrying prince's eye
sails us to the Father.

THE FACE OF CHRIST

The tragic beauty of the face of Christ
shines in the face of man;

the abandoned old live on
in shabby rooms, far from inner comfort.
Outside, in the street
din and purpose, the world like a fiery animal
reined in by youth. Within
a pallid tiring heart
shuffles about its dwelling.

Nothing, or so little, come of life's promise.
Out of broken men, despised minds
what does one make—
a roadside show, a graveyard of the heart?

The Christian God reproves
faithless ranting minds
crushing like upper and lower stones
all life between;
Christ, fowler of street and hedgerow
of cripples and the distempered old
—eyes blind as woodknots,
tongues tight as immigrants'—
takes in His gospel net
all the hue and cry of existence.

Heaven, of such imperfection,
wary, ravaged, wild?

Yes. Compel them in.

DEATHBED

Failure of action was that hour's loss.
Mind had an empyrean to attend—
angelic, cleaner than bone
it came and went, our doors and minds assaulting

with lordly assumption of eye; *you may*
if it please you, stand stolid as park statues
casting a cold shadow
on lost dogs or the rotting poor. But not I.

And so resigned the world. For what world
what hands contrived, by what means fending—

we turned aside. Like dogs or the poor, he said.

Failure of heart the last hour's loss, they said.

A Statue of the Blessed Virgin, Carven in Wood

Truly love wishes
to carve the changeful mouth to oracle,
take hand in hand
and lead her into the world. Beautiful yes
is the world, her lips would murmur,
the sweet-grained face quickening in memory

of Bethlehem or the child
her arms yearn toward, as though even we
held up a lien of innocence.

Eyes beyond reach of thirst
vindicate our hope; she descends
to shepherd girls we only hear of. Now

better to kneel under the dumb tree
that winters in her absence
but some spring, will thrust out
massive and delicate, ladders for her coming.

A Statue of the Blessed Virgin, Carven in Ivory

The herd of time riding, an intellectual
excrescence? man never was horned, until
he combated God. A serious slow prophet
descended Sinai, terrorized the query aside:

had he grown glory? were horns
cut and mortised, stone on a stone gargoyle?

Nevertheless, by way of slow
elephantine wits
such a curve time grew;
at viable tip of inauspicious starts
is you.
        The race strives to bear, a Swedish
fountain-piece, sons and daughters

upward, like waters, in hope of you.

Saint Matthew, Publican

The face on Caesar's coin
tastes no death. Turning full face
it lied, full in face. *No god but Caesar*
says the gold eye that lights, like hell
nothing to buy.

Follow Me. Superscription and its face
are sallow rust, a ruin
ignorant graves, armies, brute time
conspire toward. Caesar weeps at last
is man at last, long lives.

IRONIES

What moves me are ironies
that draw the mind free of habitual
animal ease. Sough of tides in the heart,
massive and moony, is not our sound.

But hope and despair together
bring tears to face, are a human ground;
death mask and comic, such speech
as hero and common man may coin, makes sense

contrive our face. To expunge
either, is to cast snares for the
ghost a glancing heart makes
along a ground, and airy goes its way.

BLIND MAN

Dawns that stand like chevaliers to man
and open tranquilly and in turn

stood, wooden in me: for eyes, two
driven pegs: eyes

not of glass blown, invariable
clear blue or grey, in man—but whittled, a marionette's

or mole's. *Night* my mother whispered. Her fingers
touched in stars' stead my eyes. *Day,* but no dawn.

Words, hearts, noon light, Lucifer,
love perhaps—all wear my eyes'
eyeless skin.
        And that seer shivering in deathsweat
does he have tears to spend
on his hands' botch—no eyes, no tears
for even him?

CRY

Contain me! cried stag's nostril and eye
that led their body like a smoke
through shape and shape

or a rampageous tree, that for lightning space
struck hoof to earth, and
sped was, or was tree

or a friend's eye
his beat of heart, first to last stroke—
endearing youth's shape, enduring age, a weathered hope.

Death Casts No Light on the Mind

   It is not for that; not
permeable at all, an Easter cross.

A cross to die on is plain as day.
He crossed himself, and climbed.

Now when he died there, and was lowered

the imagination springs free; it tastes
mulberries, risen tigers, Himalayas,
summer lightning—
                          the bloodstained brow
snows washed clean as amber.

Imperceptible, glacial, memory makes its world.
He leaped eternity
the whisper goes, a tiger to its prey.

SAINT JOSEPH SPEAKS

(in memoriam: Ed Willock)

1

Because I am near to you and yet not near
biblical man recedes.
A great page is not Joseph. Edify, glorify
are pluperfect, all. I send this morning
red and newborn, up—and make of yes and no,
of God and you, one interlocking hour;
parts of one heart, its red and readiness.

2

Cartwheel on cobbles
lurches along. Night is inoffensive
wind upon meadows. I hold
a few faces by heart, and of them
one, a perfection the blind moon
cannot mar, sun's fervor emulate.

Enter, love's ironies. Could love make
of two beings one, close cot door
firmly on time's face, poked fire light
one shadow at length, one consummation—what of this?

Salt tears blur the heart's text.
You hold it close in firelight, hold it at memory
seeing, not seeing. One word is all our world.

3

Prodigious Caesar rakes the village clean,
a desert garden, all of sand in waves.
The winds cast nets all night; they take
from death and Caesar, nothing.

Winter on us.
                    Wind in the belly
makes a sound like *savior*. The blind see him in air
rumor has him by heart—impregnable,
a sling, a pellet of death for Caesar's
merciless brow.
                         Starveling, chittering, envious,
the women, a driven flock.
                              But one
wan, blue as they, walks careful, grows great within.

In a foul place
shall Caesar kneel? *Sing, sing, my lady.*

4

Weathered, taciturn, that man
a miraculous life has summoned—
Heart and lathe, a serviceable
tool moderates all.

At doorway idling, you might see
bellows heat life to shape—cradle,
plowshare, coffin; man's need and passion, man.

And think idly; wood or iron he works
to something articulate and fine
shapes him too.

But no forge turns him fiery. Eyes of absolute fire
could not, snatched were they from forge
and in human face set, one unguarded

passionate moment make. Not though she
whose beauty like heliotrope turned
all day his way, pronounce

as though no other were, or newly learned
that hour, his name.

SAINT PETER SPEAKS

His guise
neither prideful nor superhuman—
a racked man
a haunted man, better;
far from false heart
and big promissory words.

Hands articulate
in stillness or action;
himself a serviceable
tool of some mystery, put by
an evening's space among men
wearily, after day's round.

Another face among faces
in twilight; out of whose body
emanations, uses of work and love
streamed like night mist
up from earth. A racked man,
a haunted man, I knew him.
If God put on a country face,
hefted man's gear, wrung
like any son, sustenance from his acre—

all were in this image,
a coloration of the human;
intent, hereditary, skillful
in man's skills; an unmistaking wit
a sense of life.

I am so mazed by courtesies
multiplied in secret, an art
of those brief years,
I had nearly forgotten
the numbed bewilderment
that stole our twelve wits
at the violent end.

Few men go crowned to death,
fewer to such death as scatters
like a wrecking trespassing king
all excellence and purpose.

I think now to recover
semblance of order
from that wilful disordered murder.

I remember vicious Tiberias sea
storming straight up
at the wind's trump.
On that green hell one face appears
clear, then sunken, nearing its peace.

He walked the storm. He made peace to be.
He summoned me, as though sea
were road and rest, Himself.
Racked man, haunted man—
the saving pain of life
was to drown out of one's human
stinking corpse,
a taken foolish fish
at wit's end drawn into being.

PHOTO

My grandmother, by time diminished
to a grandson's eye, has no word
that lights the living face to oracle.
She sits and gazes—
stillness were task enough
for a ghost's afternoon.

Breath? burdensome words?
I wonder she does not say *I love   I remember*

Her lips have nothing for us, who set great store
by love, wonder, remember.

Which to believe? in her picture, gardens
grow her ninetieth summer. At window
actual death, a January ruin.

Not Yet

I remember this;
hands of Christ laid
across man's brow and eyes.
The man of action stilled,
drawn strongly into worlds of brow,
a single vein
named thought, named love
reaming him through.

Christ and Mary know me
true grain and crooked, one.
She turning eyes from Him, as Beatrice once
bestows infrequently
a glance brimming with Christ.
And flaming souls tongue
mother and son draw near!

but here
            purgation and afar

GREAT GOD PAUSED AMONG MEN

    and spoke: *coopers, craftsmen, shepherds*
blessed is the prophet
whose blood speaks in his stead. Search death out

and sought death in their cities, and was taken
young years and all, and composed in ground
like wintering bees

and after respite stood again
to show in tremendous mime—shut doors sprung,
permeable world—all man would come to.

EVE

An old woman of hearth and field,
a husk by winter blown. Christ,
tears in the harlot's vase
are spikenard for your wounds. When women
anoint and wind and weep you,
they whisper to your hands; *Eve who is dust
bore us to your late comforting.*

THE EYES OF MAN

    not Promethean, not a wall's holy image, conceding
in nimbus or gold streamers;
temporal heats and fears
shudder a Byzantine eternity. I choose perfection in stead of
malpigmented flesh.

No, but have seen
as one rose a lovelier; altruism and sorrow,
death near, nearing that loved other.

KINDER TIMES?

> But what use were angels
in the raw world? Christ's hands and side
time hammered open.
> > They pour
human over us. Breathe deep, question his wounds
what way now?
> > Dead lips refuse all answer.

None but the chime, the synonym
made death a wine, turned all His body rose.

The Holy Innocents

Dying held no dismay.
On branches? in our mother's arms? so brief
a while to tarry. Full was her breast, sword ran too.
It might have been play; red and white
the fountain leapt—drink, then to our sleep.

Whether in foul places we lay briefly
or fleeing the fowler we sped here,
thanks to Christ whose love translated us.
Staying to learn we are but men, were word
too dull for joy at a descending sword.

Teresa of Avila

Almighty God could make again
did malice unmake the world
from my turning heart, a world of use enough.

When I ride under moon, it is
in love   in love frosty wheels tune.

Profiles, trades, brogues, oxen
milk-white, hillsides
holding, still as old shepherds, valleys of lambs—

a universe His majesty had not
foreseen? seed, pollen, world
by what gravity drawn, by wind driven,
nest in this dun body,
burr to my heart.

PARABLE

Cripples died at the poolside,
in roadways and porches. No help for it

no savior, or only one. And he passed by
or a rumor, or never was

and if by crutch or crook one stood to him—
a most unsettling genius; a rabbi of stints,

delays, deferring eyes; often
as by superior vision, futurity,

declined. No miracle in store.

There was no telling. Death kept a closed mouth.

DEATH, FRANCIS OF ANNECY

The moon, death's gentle planet,
steadies awhile at flood, a tide of sense.

Sight clouds. Half light at the lattice. He speaks
(they whisper) as though he dwelt at distance
being in enterprise of moment so caught up
as made old friends, old hands in his
unverified, arbitrary as dream.

That ivory simulacrum, his dear face!
it turns the world aside, it believes childhood.

Riding the night air
bell notes enter and crowd his sleep.

The wild stares start from eaves;
heartbeat, shape of the stilled heart, follow me.

THE SPIRITS THAT SPEAK IN US

(for *Philip*)

— What is our gift?
—Youth, heyday, age
dramatic in one mastering tree—young
for youth's sake; older, his self-sufficing thought
crowns him Lord Heaven.

— No. Parables
like your tree, root in foul earth
and suck up, even if refined to thought
a pagan stain. And he is already stained.

— But what then?

— If anything, give him what time cannot.
Paul and John breathe in our breath.
Their eternities converge, majestic
many-voiced, battering time's sail
making of life a risk, a clamorous passage
charted, chanted by spirits.

— More. Spirit is a sword, Paul said.
A sword on dexterous wrist, in dance or anger
a clear handglass makes. Among
the lightnings of that steel in air
he walks unharmed, sees and is seen.

— But will he wish to see?

— This is our gift too, the spirit self-aware.
See in the nave wall, a man of colored glass
as though the centuries were kiln
or fathering sun fervent to make one man
walks, all of fire. Man of works and days
is man at last.

— Man is a spirit? it may be, but first
consanguine, mortal, he must walk time's ruck.
And if all things unhinge, a passion
light brings on, to become light
and leap, as though life were a tree of life,
and cling, and be its fiery ornament—
still, bones are stones of men;
flesh's intent, sweet, strong by turn
clings for dear life, dear flesh. Do not abuse
or eunuch purpose with eventuality.
John and Paul live in that glass
but see, what footsteps lead man there!

— Blood. A dragged instrument of death. I see.

— If he, made infirm, cough his purpose up
that like a grit festered away false health
and sewed a jewel in rotting flesh, to wear
not here—

— If he—named Paul or John
by ordeal of waters, by drowning there
under a Hand that saved not but will save—
refuse death—

— If he refuse man, all creation
turns profitless and sour. The seasons
sodden him. Life stakes him out for show.

— How then unlearn refusal?

—He has clues
the window lights on; how time neglected
falls from myth, stones from their ordering wall,
shedding like dead heads, mortician smiles
on life.
And more, time neglected cancels eternity.
For no man stands in the wall's great wheel
where light beyond makes him perpetual dawn
had he not stood his ground, anonymous, time-worn
wearing his manhood, its coarse fabric out.

— What then be far from him? shall scorn?

— Not for scorn's opposite. You know the faults—
a slovenly priest hunching the altar side,
an abstract priest, untongued, unmanned,
a crone's heaven; a moony face on coins
blessing fat publicans, their pockets
where he fleeces.

— Legends—their priests are half a truth,
half crudity. Think rather of proud actual men
their mysteries have not made thoughtful.
A blade of mind, a blade of man, an eye
set like cold diamond in that cold;
priests a chimeric past has drowned,
dismembered, casting ashore for mock

a rusted timepiece, hands locked in vain
about some ideal unexistent hour.

—Paul knew such love of the world! he wore
the world's phylactery, its text by heart.
But sterile chastity, abstract life
are rigor mortis at the heart. They make man, Paul cried
his evil opposite, a bat-fouled steeple
shrilling blind fury if life attempt him.

— Anger is our gift then?

— In measure, yes. Angry in his shift of blood
Christ cannot die, so many soft tongues breathe
false comfort to His wounds.

— But who will wear His wounds
unhealed, their shirt of fire?

— Say it. A priest.

— A priest. So he may wear Christ's wounds
upon Christ's world,—our gift at length—
a providence the Father wrote
minuscule on Christ's flesh, in blood.

— Under time's burning-glass the text
enlarges in His eye. Good or ill,
bold-minded, neutral, priests are its capitals.

(They breathe on him. Both speak.)

— The Father's providence
written minuscule, upon flesh, with blood;
Come gospeler,
be born. Be ragman at the common stock
of ills and makeshift; improvise
oddments of life to usable frame, to voice.
But trade, trick Christ for a heart
that out of sight may royally beat and be,
a dungeon-blinded king in ecstasy.
Such light from human darkness struck
gives men their miracle: we have seen His star.

(They depart. The man, awakening, speaks.)

— For star or heart I wear, I thank you.
Man of beatific vision, first
Stands firmly in his world. Eyes at peace, hands
in saint's orante gesture, toiled once
on artefacts of man, to make the man
glass holds suspended between life and life.
At his feet, the painted tool
that once let light into dumb wood or iron
rests now, translucent as his hands. Hands, iron,
wood, man's tools and toil, have fired
eternity its frame.

(He kneels before the window.)

Burning man,
men fired and set you
to pace out upon bewildering heaven
a human city. Beckon them with the hands
whose palms men turned their way. Turn
compassionate eyes on them, true sight of those eyes
their brush deprived of Vision, as though
ignominy past, death sprung—
human eyes might hold
wine and winecup, all that shaped and filled them.